Stark County District Library
www.StarkLibrary.org
330.452.0665

MAR -- 2015

DISCARDED

W9-ALM-703

DISCOVER
Magnets

BY JULIA VOGEL • ILLUSTRATED BY JANE YAMADA

PUBLISHED by The Child's World®
1980 Lookout Drive • Mankato, MN 56003-1705
800-599-READ • www.childsworld.com

ACKNOWLEDGMENTS

The Child's World®: Mary Berendes, Publishing Director
The Design Lab: Design
Jody Jensen Shaffer: Editing
Pamela J. Mitsakos: Photo Research

PHOTO CREDITS

© Africa Studio/Shutterstock.com: 9; AntonBalazh/iStock.com: 14; Artography/
Shutterstock.com: 7; BanksPhotos/iStock.com: 11; olm26250/iStock.com: cover, 1;
Bildagentur Zoonar GmbH/Shutterstock.com: 15; Costasz/Dreamstime.com : 16;
design56/iStock.com: 17; DougSchneiderPhoto/iStock.com: 18; Imagesbybarbara/
iStock.com: 19; Maria Meester/Shutterstock.com: 6; Natali Glado/Shutterstock.
com: 8; Sergei Razvodovskij/Dreamstime.com: 5; SergeyIT/Shutterstock.com: 10;
tfoxfoto/iStock.com: 20

COPYRIGHT © 2015 by The Child's World®
All rights reserved. No part of this book may be reproduced or utilized in any form
or by any means without written permission from the publisher.

ISBN 9781626873049
LCCN 2014930656

PRINTED in the United States of America • Mankato, MN
July, 2014 • PA02220

CONTENTS

A MYSTERIOUS FORCE

You can't see it.

You can't hear it.

But it has the power to push and pull.

It's inside Earth.

It's everywhere around your home.

What is this mysterious force?

It's the power of magnets!

The force of the magnet holds these little screws tight.

WILL IT STICK?

You know that magnets stick to the fridge. Why? The door has a thin colored coating. But underneath, there's metal.

Nails have a lot of iron.
Would they stick to magnets?

Thumbtacks and needles would stick to a magnet. A piece of string would not.

Magnets **attract** certain kinds of metal. Most often, magnets stick to iron. They can also pull on other magnets.

Pennies don't scoot to a magnet. Neither does gold. Paper and pencils stay put, too. These things are not made of iron. They are not **magnetic**.

Coins are the wrong type of metal for sticking to magnets.

Things made of paper, plastic, or wood will not stick to magnets.

9

Magnets come in different sizes and shapes. Which one can pick up the most stuff? It may not be the biggest one!

Even small magnets can grab things they're not touching. Hold a refrigerator magnet above a paper clip. You can make the paper clip jump!

Paper clips stick well to this magnet.

Big magnets like this one are used in junkyards.

But what happens if you move the paper clip across the room? The trick doesn't work.

Around each magnet is an invisible space. This space is called its **magnetic field**. A magnet works only inside its magnetic field.

Scientists imagine a magnetic field as lines that loop from one end of a magnet to another. Try putting a piece of paper over a magnet. Then sprinkle the paper with small pieces of iron. The pieces will move into lines like these.

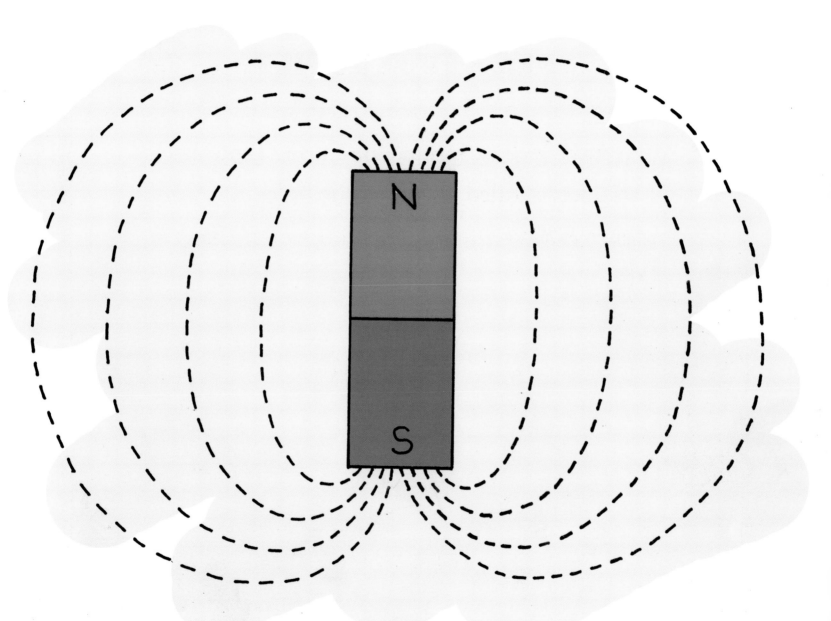

PLANET MAGNET

What's the biggest magnet on Earth? Earth itself!

Earth is a giant magnet.

You can use a compass to help you find your way. The compass needle is a magnet that always points north.

You can see Earth's power. Dangle a small bar magnet on a string. It slowly turns. One end turns north. The other end points south. The magnet is attracted to Earth.

THE POWER OF POLES

A magnet's ends have special names. The one that is attracted to Earth's northern tip is called the north **pole**. The other end is the south pole.

A magnet's power is strongest at its poles. But it works only in certain ways.

A magnet's poles are marked with N and S.

The opposite poles on two magnets attract.

Line up two bar magnets like train cars. Do the ends pull together? If so, you've matched the north and south poles. Opposite poles attract.

What if the ends push apart? That means you've matched north with north or south with south. Poles that are alike **repel**. They push each other apart.

These toy train cars are connected by magnets. If you turned the last car of this train around, it would not stick to the middle car.

MAGNETS EVERY DAY

Did you use a computer today? Did you talk on the phone? If so, you were using the power of magnets. Magnets are important parts of many machines.

Many magnets are **electromagnets**. Electricity makes them strong. A powerful electromagnet can pick up a car! What else can magnets do? Test it yourself with magnets!

This electromagnet is used in a scrapyard.

MORE MAGNET MAGIC

The door of your refrigerator is probably coated with plastic.
But you can still use a magnet to stick artwork on it, right?
That's because magnets can work through certain materials.
Here's a list of a few things that let magnetic force through.

glass	cloth
air	plastic
paper	water

GLOSSARY

attract (uh-TRAKT): To attract is to pull together. Opposite poles on a magnet attract.

electromagnet (eh-LEK-tro-MAG-net): An electromagnet is a magnet that is made with electricity. An electromagnet can be very powerful.

magnetic (mag-NET-ik): Magnetic things will stick to a magnet. Magnetic objects most likely have a lot of iron in them.

magnetic field (mag-NET-ik FEELD): A magnetic field is the space around a magnet where the magnet works. The more powerful the magnet is, the stronger its magnetic field.

poles (POHLZ): Poles are ends of a magnet, where its power is strongest. One end is called the north pole, and the other is the south pole.

repel (ruh-PEHL): To repel is to push away. Alike poles on a magnet repel.

TO LEARN MORE

In the Library

Branley, Franklyn Mansfield. *What Makes a Magnet?* New York: HarperCollins, 1996.

Schreiber, Anne. *Magnets*. New York: Grosset & Dunlap, 2003.

Silverman, Buffy. *Magnet Power*. Vero Beach, FL: Rourke, 2012.

On the Web

Visit our Web site for lots of links about Magnets:

www.childsworld.com/links

Note to Parents, Teachers, and Librarians: We routinely check our Web links to make sure they're safe, active sites—so encourage your readers to check them out!

INDEX

3 1333 04390 9736